101 Frugal Tips

How to save money and live a minimalistic life

DIANE ROSE

DIANE ROSE

ISBN: 1514888106
ISBN-13: 9781514888100

101 Frugal Tips -How to save money and live a minimalistic life is dedicated to an anonymous person in my distant past that inspired me to write this booklet many moons ago. Though we are no longer in contact anymore, nor will ever be. Thank you sir!

I cannot forget the patience of my two children while Mom is brainstorming and writing. I love you, Mnason and Laban.

DIANE ROSE

TABLE OF CONTENTS

BEING FRUGAL

The word frugal is defined from the *Webster's New Universal Unabridged Dictionary* as this: "Economical in use or expenditure; prudently saving or sparing; entailing little expense; requiring few resources; meager; scanty."

Frugalness is using whatever possessions you have on hand and utilizing them to make another way. Therefore, the essence of being frugal is using your imagination to invent or change your possessions into something else. Others may perceive this as being cheap or eccentric; others see it as being frugal, inventive, and innovative. Some people would rather go to the store to buy something new, but why would you go to the store when often times you are able to resolve the problem by being frugal or otherwise creative at home?

Personally, living frugal or being frugal is taking $50 to a grocery store and using it to feed a household (of four) for a week or more, ensuring nutrition and variance is considered when purchasing each meal. The value of the various components of each meal can be assessed through the nutritional value and not through the price tags attached. The value of each dollar spent on the ingredients of each meal prepared is whether the meal is satiating and not whether it cost a fortune to prepare. A dollar is relative and should not be seen as the true value for any commodity, but from the utility that is derived from using the said commodity.

I have been accused of being too frugal or cheap by various family members. I shop regularly at dollar stores and thrift stores. I think that I am often getting great bargains at those two places. The dollar stores provide useful items for an everyday price of a single dollar (or sometimes even less). For example, why spend $10 for a candle elsewhere when at a dollar store, it's about $2? Especially since these two candles will perform the same task– burn to the wick!

Frugality is a common daily task or idea for me. I like to spend money, but only on items that I think that are worth my dollar. Most times these items are necessities and I buy a certain brand– especially when it is on sale. Some of these items are: toilet paper (Scotts), deodorant (Dove),

magazines (Essence, Woman's Day, and Family Circle),

sanitary napkins (Always),

jam or jelly (Smuckers),

tea (Celestial Seasonings Quietly Chamomile),

ice cream (Breyers or Ben and Jerry's),

bath soap (Ivory),

cookies (Pepperidge Farm, Oreos, or Chip Ahoy),

peanuts (Planter's),

etc.

I have laid out the frugal ways in an alphabetical order to better assist you in the areas needed in your life:

√ Apps

√ Children

√ Clothes

√ Cooking

√ Decorating

√ Entertainment

√ Home

√ Internet

√ Miscellaneous

√ Money

√   Shopping.

To aid in being frugal, I have also included two useful tools. How to create a Simple Budget will help to create an easy way to track monthly income and expenses for an entire year to show where your money is being used. The 365 Days Penny Savings Challenge will show how to save a penny a day to achieve close to $700 in one year. Happy savings!

APPS

DealNews.com Black Friday (iOS, Android; free)

On Black Friday, the best deals go on sale early and sell out within minutes. Save time and money by planning for shopping in advance by using the DealNews.com Black Friday app. The app collects all the Black Friday sales in a format that is easy to navigate; you can save individual items to your shopping list and even view a price comparison to help to decide if that is really a bargain worth braving the crowds for later on.

eBay Mobile (iOS, Android, Windows Phone, BlackBerry; free)

eBay Mobile is useful if you are an active bidder on auctions. The app notifies you of outbids or if an auction that is being followed is about to close. The interface is simple but robust, making it painless to bid on or create auctions directly from your mobile phone.

GeoQpons (iOS, Android, BlackBerry; free)

GeoQpons is a deal-finding app that searches

coupons based on your ZIP code and sorts them by offers from major retailers and local businesses. Local deals are not limited to retailers; there are also other services listed, such as salons, spas, and restaurants. Most coupons can be scanned directly from the phone; however, the app will display a warning notification for any deals that may require printing out the coupon(s).

PriceGrabber (iOS, Android; free)

PriceGrabber is the mobile extension of the popular shopping comparison website and it works just as well. First, enter the product for purchase, and the app pulls up a list of stores carrying the item along with pricing information for comparison, local deals (when available), and a product description. Other features include the Gift Shaker; a gift randomizer which allows you to specify a category and price range and displays potential gift items that match, along with a bar code scanner for quickly locating a product.

Red Laser (iOS, Android, Windows Phone; free)

When comparing prices between a store and the

Internet, you have to look for the item in person, then go home and manually search for a better price online. To use this app, scan the bar code or QR code with RedLaser and within a few seconds there is a well-organized list of locations and prices to choose from. If you don't have a bar code to scan, you can also find products by keyword by taking a photo of the item and performing a reverse image search.

RetailMeNot (iOS, Android; free)

If you use the website RetailMeNot, the app version is just as useful. It provides a comprehensive list of stores with both online and in-store coupons, along with coupon expiration dates, and user comments. It's easy to find deals based on your ZIP code, and in-store coupons can be redeemed directly from your mobile phone.

CHILDREN

Audio Books

Record your own voice, or a much-loved family member's voice, on tapes or CDs reading to your children. Story time will be great and familiar when you are not present. This prevents separation, especially if your spouse is in the military or works odd hours at their job. Make sure to have a picture of the person reading the audio book close to the child so that he or she remembers who the person is reading. If you are pressed for time, Hallmark has audiobooks for about $10 in the children's stories section.

Baby Food

Make your own baby food instead of using canned or bottled food. Use fresh fruits and vegetables; steam them until they are mushy or a little less than crunchy. Mash them with a potato masher or use a food processor to puree. Feed the mixture to your child when cooled, or freeze in ice-cube trays covered with plastic wrap. When ready to serve (by cubes), thaw at room temperature, and presto, you have a meal in minutes!

Breast Feeding

Breast fed babies are more easily weaned and weaned even sooner than their counterparts; bottle fed babies. They don't have digestive problems that plague bottle fed babies (constipation, indigestion, etc.) and they're generally healthier too. You can save up to $1000 per year this way. It is easier to extract milk from a breast rather than sterilize a bottle, heat milk or water, and mix with formula. The cheapest way is the easiest way in this case!

Building Blocks

Instead of throwing old building blocks out, decorate handles or draw pulls in a children's room with old or mismatched building blocks that are left over from when the child was a toddler.

Child Care

Instead of paying for child care when you go out for a night on the town, ask your neighbor or a relative to baby sit for you. Return the favor whenever this person wants to go out. This can be turned into a babysitting co-op. A baby sitting co-op is a network of mothers and fathers joining together to offer childcare to each other on points to points basis.

Cloth Diapers

If you are a stay at home mom, use cloth diapers instead of disposable ones (unless you are going out or it is night time). Cloth diapers may be expensive in the beginning, but it will be cheaper and more environmentally friendly in the end. Non-cloth diapers cannot be properly disposed of because of their material content.

Pre-moistened Towelettes/Wipes

Make your own pre-moistened towelettes/wipes by soaking paper towels in a mixture of a few tablespoons of baby oil mixed with one cup of soapy water. Store the pre-moistened towelettes/wipes in a plastic bag. Use for the nursery or for quick household cleaning.

Rechargeable Batteries

Most children toys use batteries. It is cost efficient to

buy rechargeable batteries in different sizes along with the charger. This can be used to power children's toys at a cheaper cost than purchasing regular, new batteries every time regular batteries are out of power. Rechargeable batteries can also be used to power electronics, especially those that are used more often in your house, like remote controls. Just remember to also recharge the batteries!

Toys

Use the $1 dollar store to buy stuffed animals and toys for children. Check parts and labeling first for safety (especially if there is a lead content) and age-appropriate reasons. In case your child is a bit destructive, you will not feel the strain on your pockets from buying toys for an expensive amount of money.

CLOTHES

Accessories

Scarves, brooches, and pins (some handmade) can be used to jazz up an outfit. To make handmade brooches and pins, buy pin backs from the craft store and glue paper or pasta pieces to it (make sure that you have decorated the pins to match your wardrobe). These can also be purchased from your local beauty supply store.

Buying

Do not buy any clothing unless it is on sale. Just wait for a week or two and that blouse you saw will be on sale by then. Most stores usually have a sale a week or two after an item has been in the store.

Clearance

At the end of different seasons, stores normally mark down newly out of season items up to 75% off their original prices. Buy clothing for the next year ahead of time on clearance. For children, purchase their winter wardrobe for next season at the end of this winter season, and so on. Remember to purchase the clothes a size or two larger to accommodate your child's growth. There is always a clearance rack in department stores. You can find out of season and deep sale items on the clearance rack. The clearance rack is normally located towards the rear of the store or at the back of different departments.

Clothes in Style or Fashion

Never buy clothes in fashion at any particular time since most styles are just passing fads. Instead, buy staple clothes that can be worn for the next two seasons or until they are worn out. Stick with the basics. For example, it is fashion right now to wear booty hugging shorts, come next summer it will be out of fashion. Buy sturdy shorts (preferable walking ones) that can be worn throughout the year or for many seasons. You can always be sure your clothing styles will last from year to year when you buy perennial standbys such as medium length, A-line skirts and solid, tailored blazers for women or neutral color shirts and tailored to semi-tailored sports coats for men.

Consignment/Resale Shops

Consignment shops can be a great place for clothes

bought for occasions that might never be worn again, such as fancy evening gowns. Give this gown to a clothing consignment shop where you can make some money. Clothing consignment shops hold and sell your clothes, and then give you a percentage of the selling price. You might be thinking that you had wasted your money on that gown. Look at it this way, which way is money being wasted; having the gown sitting in your closet collecting dust or getting a percentage of the sale price for it?

Hand-me Downs

Wear your older sibling's clothes or vice versa. This is great for adults and children. If the clothes are sturdy, pass them along to a younger sibling. This is just like purchasing clothes from the Thrift Store only in this case, you know who wore the clothes before you.

Old Things to New things

If you do not donate to Thrift Stores or use your clothes as hand-me downs, turn them into something useful and "new" to you. Old shirts can be turned into dish rags, also old pants and jeans can be turned into new skirts or purses.

Pantyhose

Wear pantyhose that are a size or two bigger than what size you would normally wear. This prevent a lot of stretching and they will last longer than if you would have worn a regular fit.

Sales Rack

Always use the sales rack at major department stores. The sales rack is usually located in the back of the store (next to the clearance rack). You should only pay full price in a major department store ONLY if the article of clothing is of good quality and will be able to transform from occasion to occasion.

Separates

If you can, buy most of your work clothes in separates. Mixing and matching your clothes- such as blouses, sweaters, skirts, pants, vests, and blazers- makes for a lot of different outfits. Buy all your basics pieces (skirts, pants, and blazers) in neutral colors and traditional styles. Then, buy trendy colors in your other clothes- blouses, sweaters, scarves, etc., that will go with all of your neutral pieces.

Sewing

If you have the time, learn to make your own clothing. When you learn to sew, you can make or fashion any piece of material into a lovely outfit. Buying patterns from hobby shops will teach you how to cut and sew the staple pieces needed for your wardrobe. Imagine making yourself a great outfit for only $5.00 (material, thread, and buttons included). Discount fabrics can easily be found at garage sales or the sales bin at any hobby shop. These can be used to make your new clothing from.

Versatility

Wear or buy clothing that can be used for more than one occasion. For example, some scarves that are big enough can be worn as halter tops or as wide belts.

COOKING/FOOD

Bakery Outlets

Bakery Outlets, bread manufacturer's outlets, or thrift stores are stores that are manned by a bakery to discount their products. In stock you can find bread, muffins, and sometimes even tortillas, depending on what the bakery makes. The prices there are generally lower than purchasing from your regular neighborhood grocer. Be warned, though, sometimes the expiration dates on the products are usually sooner than those at the grocery store!

Batch Cooking

Do larger portions when cooking. Batch cooking can be achieved simply by doubling the ingredients in your recipe, then cooking them in sets. Store the batches or excess portions in freezable containers or in bags. This can be seen as convenience food for times when you either do not want to cook or when friends drop by unexpectedly.

Brand name and Generic

These can be mixed together to create both the taste

of the brand name for a lower cost and a longer shelf life. For example, cereals can be mixed together for an interesting and great taste. Most generic cereals are available in plastic bags as opposed to brand name cereals that are packaged in well-designed boxes. However, the cost of both will be different, not necessarily because of taste, but because of the cost of the packaging itself and the brand name.

Bread and Bread Ends

Save old bread and/or bread ends in a bag in the freezer, keep adding to it until there is almost a loaf. Crumb in a blender or food processor or by hand with a grate, season with your favorite seasonings, and store them in the freezer until you need bread crumbs.

Use the breadcrumbs as stuffing mix or as mixes to roll meat items in that are going to be either fried or baked. Add butter and water to the breadcrumbs. Heat the mixture in the microwave, and serve for a quick meal idea.

Bulk Buying

Buy food items (dry or canned food items) in bulk, then separate into smaller portions for day-to-day usage. This can be done for meat, large canned items, pancake mixes, rice, flour, and sugar.

Butter or Margarine Wrappers

Save and freeze butter or margarine wrappers. These wrappers can be used to grease baking containers (dishes or pans) before baking items.

Casseroles

Use leftover meat, pasta, and/or vegetables (preferably frozen) to make casseroles with. Add leftover meat, pasta, and vegetables, mix together with cheese or tomato sauce, and top with either bread crumbs or more cheese. Bake. This will make for a very tasty meal.

Dry Pasta

Buy a lot of dry pasta. Many meals can be made with pasta as the base. Pasta can be made into one pot nutritious meals or casseroles, complete with meat, vegetables, and the pasta as a starch. Some suggestions are: cold pasta salad (any cooked pasta drained and cooled mixed with frozen vegetables, diced cheese, mayonnaise, salt, and pepper), pasta casserole (cooked pasta baked with leftover meats, vegetables, and sauce), pasta and vegetables (cooked and drained pasta mixed with cooked from frozen vegetables).

Frozen Vegetables

Frozen vegetables are as versatile as dry pasta is. They can also be used in some dishes that include dry pasta. These are not as good as using fresh vegetables, but who knows how fresh the vegetables in the produce section of grocery stores really are? Frozen vegetables can be added to rice to make a rice and vegetables meal. Frozen vegetables can also be added to mashed potatoes to make a meal seem larger.

Ground Meat

Ground meat is another versatile staple. It can use for homemade hamburgers, chilies, casseroles, sandwiches, or meat sauces.

Iced Tea

Brew iced tea from tea bags instead of buying instant ice tea. Instant iced tea is more expensive than buying a box of tea bags. Flavors can be enhanced by adding any of the following: Kool-Aid, sugar, honey, or sliced fruits (apples, lemon/lime, or orange slices). Freeze leftover iced tea in ice cube trays. This makes a flavorful addition to your drink instead of using plain ice, which water down your drinks in the end.

Kool-Aid Mixes

Kool-Aid Mixes can be used instead of sodas and pre-made bought drinks. It is cheaper to make a gallon of Kool-Aid than to buy a liter of soda.

Lunch Boxes/Brown Bags

Prepare lunches ahead of time (preferably the night before while serving dinner) for both children and adult lunches. Use reusable bags or Ziploc bags to pack your lunches in.

Meatless Meals

Plan at least one meatless meal per week. This helps make your grocery bill dramatically cheaper. You can save a lot of money by going meatless. Some ideas are: vegetarian lasagna, casseroles, quesadillas, and beans and rice.

Milk Substitute

If you have to use milk, use the cheapest brand or use powdered milk. Powdered milk will last longer (no expiration date) than regular milk will and it can be used in the same fashion as regular milk.

Salad Dressing

This is the oldest salad dressing known; oil and vinegar. Use 1 part oil (Olive, Corn, etc.) to 1 part vinegar (plain old White Cane or flavored). You can also add cracked black pepper and parsley to give it some pep. Store the mixture in the refrigerator in a jar or reuse a salad dressing bottle.

Store Brand

Buy store brand when shopping at the grocery store. Store brands also go on sale just like name brands do. Some stores will even print coupons for their brands and publish them in their weekly coupon circulars. Store brands are usually available for almost all products.

Tomato Paste and Sauces

Use tomato pastes and tomato sauces to make your

own pasta sauces instead of buying bottled sauces. Thin tomato paste with water, add garlic powder and dried oregano to make homemade tomato sauce.

Water Purifier

Never use a water purifier, just boil your tap water, let it cool, and store it in the refrigerator as drinking water. When water is boiled 98% of the bacteria is eliminated, therefore making it safer to drink.

DECORATING

Artwork

Use old postcards (or other cards) as artwork. Frame these and hang them on your wall. There are beautiful postcards available at antique stores or museum shops. Also use cards that are sentimental to you, like birthday cards, or postcards from places that you have visited, etc. An inexpensive frame and a mat that matches your room décor (use leftover cardstock or construction paper for the mat), and then assemble. Now you have a timeless piece that possibly cost you about $3 to create.

Buy inexpensive frames or framed pictures from Dollar Stores or garage/yard sales. Use construction paper as matting. Put together copied or enlarged pictures of your children, pets, or dried flowers (place fresh flowers or leaves between pages of telephone directory for a few days until it has reached the desired pressed features). This will turn out to be a priceless piece of art.

Use calendars (after the New Year, it is much cheaper) or get them from places of business (around the Christmas Holidays) as artwork. Use the pictures from them as artwork for your walls. You can find calendars with animals and lovely flowers. Again, an inexpensive frame can be used with a border that matches your room décor (use leftover cardstock or construction paper for border), and then assemble. Instant artwork!

Candles

Candles will go a long way to make a home feel cozy during the day or at night. Buy pretty candle holders made of glass at your local dollar store or chain store. Buy a large pack of tea light candles and display them in the holders all over your home. This will bring added warmth to your home and make your home feel extra special. This will also lower your electricity bill if you use the candles at nighttime instead of lights.

Canning Jars and Vases

Fill old canning jars with beans, pasta, popcorn, or marbles. Display them in the kitchen, on a dresser, table, or on top of the mantle.

Children's Drawing

Use your young children's artwork as decorations for your wall. Place them in an inexpensive frame using your leftover construction paper or cardstock as mats for them.

Decorating Tips for a Room

Mirrors will help to enlarge and brighten a room. Use sample soaps or scented perfume sample ads from a magazine or department store mailing that you have received, place them in drawers to give them a nice smell.

Paint gives walls a new, different, or exciting new look to them.

Stenciled and wallpapered borders give rooms a new life.

Blankets, throw pillows, and colorful throws brighten up a room.

Brighten and cover your old-looking accent pillows with sewn on buttons.

Potted plants and large framed photographs can both be used as accents in a room.

Large Canisters

Decorate large canisters, such as oatmeal containers, with leftover wrapping paper, pictures, or pictures from old magazines. Use these as a storage spot for pens and pencils or use it as holder for dried or silk flowers.

Plates, Cups, and Saucers (Crockery)

Do not keep your best China or crockery locked away somewhere. Display them! Parade your teapots or pretty cups and saucers or special plates in a grouping on either a mantle or table.

ENTERTAINMENT

Cable

If you live in a metropolitan area, there is enough entertainment on regular TV without the need for cable. Public Television has a variety of programs to offer, ranging from cartoons to movies.

CDs

Find stores that allow you to listen to CDs first before you purchase them (again, this is probably in a used CD store) so you will not pay 20 dollars on a CD that ends up not being to your liking. Borrowing the CD from a friend prior to purchasing a CD or buying a used CD can save the listener the grief of having purchased the CD and not liking it. Purchase songs online through places such as www.itunes.com or www.amazon.com instead of purchasing an entire album as well.

Community Newspaper

Community Newspapers always have listings for free concerts, museum visits, and other such cultural events. These newspapers are usually free at your local grocery stores or other local businesses.

Department of Tourism/ Parks Department

Most cities' Department of Tourism/Parks
Department plan and offer free or low-cost events.
Call them to find out about free festivals, outdoor
movies, concerts, plays, craft festivals, etc.

Eating Out

When eating out, eat lunch instead of dinner.
Prices at most restaurants are significantly lower
for lunch with the same amounts per serving as
if it were dinner.

If you have to eat dessert, eat it somewhere
other than at the restaurant. Desserts at
restaurants are often overpriced. If you do
choose to have dessert at a restaurant, share it
with your dinner partner so that the cost is also
shared.

Drink water, sodas, or iced tea. Water is always free!
Sodas and iced teas are often refillable.

Check local coupons sites for deals at local
restaurants, bars, or pubs. Generally, a dinner for

two can be purchased for the price of one on these sites.

Library

Use your local library for entertainment purposes. Some libraries have magazines, newspapers, CDs, DVDs, and audio tapes or books, or even VHS tapes for loan that is lower than a movie rental or movie purchase from your cable company.

Use the library for your internet needs. You can use the library's computers and printers or even use your own laptop with the library's WIFI access at no cost to you. (Usually, you only have to pay for the pages that are printed through the library's printers.)

Magazines

Some of the most popular magazines have websites. Visit the magazines' websites instead of paying for a subscription. Sometimes the website will not have all the articles that are in the print version. But would you rather pay for a paper version with all the articles rather than have a free version with limited articles?

You can also check out copies of magazines at some libraries.

Movies

Only see movies in theaters that you really want to see. If not, wait until the movie has reached cable, network TV, $1/$3 Theater, or video rentals.

Museums

Some museums offer free visits, some even offer free full days for the entire family.

Non-Stingy Dates

Go on of dates with people that are not tightfisted. They will pay for the entire meal and other entertainment without asking to go dutch.

$1/$3 Theater

Most major cities have theaters that let you pay a minimal sum (usually $1/$3) to see a movie that has already been in major movie theaters for a while. This is not offered in all states.

HOME

Butter or Whipped Cream Containers/Jars

Reuse jars as storage containers for small things or to store homemade sauces. Clean and sanitize the jars first if you are planning on using it as a storage container for food items.

Save these containers and use them to store leftovers, small items, children's barrettes, etc. These containers are able to store items in the kitchen. They were made for having more than one function.

Candle Holders

Save your candle holders even after the candle has burnt out. Clean the candle holders and buy candles in the grocery store for $1 for 3 candles. Place the new candles in the holder. Now you have new candles in holders.

Cleaning Spray Bottles

Use old spray bottles for new stuff. When you buy spray bottles, like bathroom cleaners, do not throw them out when they are finished. Wash them out properly and fill them with a cleaning solution of half bleach or ammonia and half water. Use this solution for cleaning anything– the bathroom and kitchen surfaces. Remember to always relabel these bottles with their new contents, though.

Dishwasher

Use a dishwasher only when it is completely full. You will both conserve energy and save water this way. Instead of using the dishwasher when it is half-empty, wash the dishes by hand. If you do not have a dish washer, fill the sink with water to wash the dishes. If equipped with two sides of a sink, fill one side with soap and water to wash the dishes with and the other side with clean water to rinse the dishes. This will save you a lot on water usage.

Dryer Sheets (Fabric Softener Sheets)

These can be used as a refresher by placing fresh sheets between clothes in drawers, in closets, and under garbage bags in cans.
Use old dryer sheets to dust your furniture and blinds with. The static from the sheets will cling to the dust and lift it right off your furniture and blinds. Use old dryer sheets to wipe the lint screen of your dryer and to get pet hair off of surfaces.

Use old dryer sheets to eliminate static cling in your skirts by rubbing on the dryer sheets on your pantyhose.

Use fresh dryer sheets dipped in water to remove bugs, particularly love bugs, which can embed themselves on the grill, hood, and windshield of your vehicles.

Eliminate Odors

Baking soda will eliminate odors by destroying odors safely and naturally. It can also be used to keep odors from the refrigerator. To eliminate odors from a trash can, litter boxes, or your clothes hamper, sprinkle some baking soda in the receptacle.

Baking soda can also be poured down the kitchen drain to eliminate odors there. After pouring it down the drain, let the hot water run for about a minute or more.

Garbage Disposal

After eating an orange or any other citric fruit, put the peel of it in the garbage disposal, run hot water, and turn the disposal on. This will leave the kitchen smelling like citrus and hopefully help with unclogging your drain in the process.

Laundry

Use less laundry detergent than the manufacture
calls for on the packaging.
Add baking soda and/or plain vinegar to laundry to
make the laundry smell fresher and cleaner.
Wash clothes in cold water to save energy, especially
dark-colored clothes which tend to bleed in the
laundry.

Light Bulbs

Replace your regular incandescent bulbs with
compact fluorescent. They use less energy for the
same amount of light, and give off less heat, and will
last longer than ordinary incandescent bulbs. A 23
watt compact fluorescent bulb gives off the same
amount of light as a single 100 watt incandescent
bulb. You might check with your local electricity
company to see if they are offering any types of
rebates for using fluorescent bulbs in your house.

Liquid Hand Soap

To make liquid hand soap; add 1 bar of soap, small
(not super-sized) to 3 cups of water. Grate the bar of
soap with a cheese grater. Pour the water and grated

soap into a microwaveable container and cook the mixture on high for 3 minutes. Remove the mixture and stir until all the soap bits have melted (you can put it in the microwave a bit longer, if needed). Let it cool, then pour into pumps (leftover from store bought liquid soap), and put the remainder in any container with a lid. This makes about 24 oz.

Mesh Onion Bags

Use these to wash pots and pans by using it as a pot scrubber or scouring pad. Crush the mesh bag together and bind with a rubber band then scrub away!

Old Socks

Use old socks as furniture or window blinds cleaner. Stick your hand in the sock, apply polish or cleaner to it, and clean your surfaces. It is just like wiping the surface with your hands! Use a pair, one for dusting and the other one for cleaning.

Place Mats

Clear contact paper can be used as place mats. Peel one sheet of contact paper, put it sticky side up on top of a flat surface, and place dried leaves (or paper shapes or felt pieces) on it. Peel another sheet of contact paper and place the sticky side down on top of the first piece. Repeat the process three other times. Now you have a new set of place mats!

Reuse and Recycle

Reuse and recycle Ziploc bags, wrapping paper, aluminum foil, plastic and paper bags, baby food containers, and other types of containers (these can be used primarily for storage). Wash and sanitize these items before reusing so as not to contaminate the food that will be put into these containers with the previous contents.

Recycle small grocery bags and use them as thrash bags especially in small trash cans.

Saving Energy

When you are not at home, turn off your AC or Heater, or put them on a lower/higher setting to save energy.

Soiled Tablecloths

Make old or soiled tablecloths into table runners, place mats, napkins, or kitchen towels.

Towels

Old towels make great cleaning cloths, small washrags (just sew the edges together), and hand towels (also sewn together).

White Cane Vinegar

White Cane Vinegar can be used for many different purposes. It can be used as a cleaning agent, odor eliminator, and for cleaning meat, poultry, and fruit. Use it to clean out coffee pots, stoves, microwaves, floors, bathtubs, and even counter tops.

To use it as an odor eliminator, put about a cup in a microwaveable bowl and microwave it for about two minutes and leave in an open place. The smell is vinegary at first, but after the smell goes away, odors such as pet urine or fried foods will be all gone.

Window Cleaner

Windshield cleaner fluid that is used for automobiles can also be used as a household window cleaner. It is cheaper than commercial window cleaner is and it does the same job at a cheaper cost.

INTERNET

AOL

AOL Internet Service Provider is too expensive, if you have it, cancel it. Try another provider, such as NetZero or Juno, the services are similar to AOL but the prices are about $10 less.

www.coolsavings.com

This is a great site for the shopper in all of us. Use it to download and print grocery, store, or online coupons; receive gift certificates or rebates; price comparison; and also receive free samples from top name brands.

www.ebay.com

Use eBay to bid on things that you must have but cannot afford at their full price. However, you can always cancel your bidding before it goes beyond your budget.

Email

Get a free email account at www.hotmail.com,

www.gmail.com or www.yahoo.com. Check your email messages from these websites from any remote location by just logging onto that site, instead of using an email account that there is a fee to pay to view messages.

www.half.com

Buy, sell, and/or trade old books, CDs, video games, computers, electronics, and movies at this site. Textbooks are even available at prices that are significantly lower than they are college bookstores.

Instant Messenger

Instead of relying on an AOL account for an instant messenger, either download a free AOL instant messenger or download a free one from AT&T. The AT&T IM is great because by using that one IM, there is access to Yahoo IM, AOL IM, and MSN Messenger. So instead of having all three instant messengers running at one time, there is only one running with all three services automatically included.

www.LowerMyBills.com

Use this site to lower your utility bills by comparing low rates on those bills which in turn reduce your cost of living. These monthly bills can include home loans, credit cards, auto and health insurance, and long distance and wireless services.

www.mypoints.com

Use MyPoints to earn rewards simply by reading advertisements from emails, shopping online, and touring web sites after signing up for free. Redeem your points for gift certificates to different stores, such as Kmart, Target, Barnes & Noble, etc.

www.netflix.com

If you and your family are into movies, try using Netflix. This is an online DVD rental club and/or streaming club that offers unlimited DVD rentals for about $20 per month and/or streaming movies for about $10 per month. It works by choosing up to three movies online that will be delivered to your door in approximately three days' time. Enclosed is an envelope which allows the customer the privilege of returning the movies once viewed without the cost of shipping and handling. There are no late fees and no limits on membership. The streaming movies can be selected and viewed on almost any internet ready devices.

www.stretcher.com

The Dollar Stretcher is THE original resource for ideas on saving money in various areas of your daily life. There are frugal ideas there ranging from automobile expenses, financing, budgeting, and couponing.

www.valupage.com

Use ValuPage when going to the grocery store. There is no sign up page for this site. Enter your local ZIP code, select the supermarket of your choice, and print your ValuPage shopping list. While at the supermarket, buy one or more items that are listed on your ValuPage shopping list, give this list to the cashier right before checking out, and receive Get ValuPage Savings to purchase anything on the next visit to the grocery store.

www.vistaprint.com

Vistaprint is very versatile for printed materials and other items, such as tote bags and t-shirts. It is very inexpensive also, you can order custom printed business cards (usually 250) for about $10. But this small, minimal fee is used for shipping and handling. In essence, those cards are yours for free. Meanwhile a local printer will charge you about $50 for 100 basic business cards.

MISCELLANEOUS

Batteries

Radio Shack offers, at no charge, a battery card to its customers. Each time batteries are purchased, the customer is eligible to receive free batteries after the fifth or sixth purchase.

Beauty School

If you are in close proximity to a beauty school, use the school for hair and sometimes, nails and makeup needs. They are generally cheaper than a salon and usually there is no tipping included for the work done there. After all, these students are practicing their craft for a nominal fee.

Gas

There are a number of ways that you can save on gas. Run all errands once a week to save from driving to and fro daily.

Use a discount card to buy gas. Winn-Dixie, Walmart, and Sam's Club offer members a discount or percentage off on gas at theirs or different service stations. Fill your tank up early in the morning, when the air is cool and gas is dense. There will be more gas in your tank but less air.

Fill up your car when the tank is half-full. Again, more gas, less air!

Gift Giving

Gift Mixes in a Jar: These are easy to make and inexpensive. Just about anything can be made 'in a jar'. For instance: Milk Bath in a Jar, Hot Spiced Wine Mix in a Jar, Chocolate Chip Cookies in a Jar, French Vanilla Cocoa Mix in a Jar, Red Beans And Rice Mix in a Jar, Cinnamon-Oat Pancakes in a Jar. The ingredients can be altered to make low-fat, low-salt, or diabetic mixes. To make a simple gift mix in a jar: use your favorite baking recipe, layer the dry ingredients in a jar, write instructions on a tag and attach it to the jar. (Remember to include the wet ingredients for the baking recipe on the tag also.)

Themed Gift Baskets: Baskets can be bought throughout the year at garage sales and flea markets, then painted and decorated. Customize the gift basket to the person who is going to be receiving it, for instance; a chocolate lover will love a basket that contains cookies, chocolate covered popcorn, nuts, and a hot chocolate mix. Gift Certificates or Gift Cards: If you do not know what a person might or might not want, get them a gift certificate or a gift card. Gift cards can be generic, such as an American Express gift card, but they can also be custom, such as a gift card to a favorite store of the receiver of the gift.

Scented Soaps: Use your ingenuity and make custom scented soaps. Buy bulk glycerin soap and essential oils to make the soaps with. Melt the glycerin soap and add some essential oil. Pour the mixture into molds. Unmold and wrap. Other items can also be added to the soap, such as: oatmeal, flower petals, colored soap chips, and loofah sponge.

Hobby

Start a hobby. A hobby can be something that you do or share with your family or friends. Your family or friends can pool resources so that it is cost efficient. This is a cheaper thing to do with your time than going shopping. You will be happy with the end result of your new hobby!

Hot Water Bottle

A soda bottle (preferably a 1 liter bottle) can be used as a hot water bottle. Put water that has been heated in the bottle, then wrap the bottle in a hand towel, then place it on the area that needs pain relief.

Long Distance Carriers and Credit Cards

Long Distance Carriers and Credit Cards usually lower their rates if you tell them that you are planning on leaving. Tell them the name of the new company that you are going to and the rates that they are offering and the company that you are with will either lower your rate or will "find" other plans or ways to encourage you to stay with them.

Medication

Ask your pharmacist for generic brands for your brand name medications. Generic brands are usually just the same as name brands with the same basic ingredients, just with a slight difference, maybe, in color, shape, or taste. The uses and effects should also work the same as your name brand medications.

Buy generic medication at Walmart or Target. They have a lot of different medications available for only $4.

Newspaper

Use shredded newspaper as mulch in the garden. This can also be used instead of kitty litter. Newspaper keeps the smell of the litter to a minimum. Remember to dump the newspaper weekly.

Shredded newspaper can also be used as packaging material when sending packages through the mail. Instead of buying special paper to wrap items in the mail, shredded newspaper can be used for cushioning.

Newspaper can also be used to wrap glasses and other fragile items in the home when packing to move or for storage purposes.

Pet Home

If there is a small dog or cat in the home, use a play pen as a house for the pet. Find a play pen at the Thrift store or at a yard sale, line it with paper (preferably newspaper) and this will be a pen small enough for inside the home but large enough for the small pet.

Prepaid Telephones

If there is a need for a cellular telephone plan, but there is no need for you to have a cellular telephone except only for emergencies, then TracFone is for you. There is a wireless service offered for about $8 a month including voice mail and caller ID. TracFone prepaid telephones can be found in local corner stores, Wal-Mart, or Staples for about $10 including a cellular telephone and an airtime card.

Presents

Buy presents when they are on sale or before the holidays or any other special occasions. This will avoid additional charges that stores will add on to accompany the holidays.

School

Practical or career schools offer inexpensive services. Local colleges offer dental work, nail and hair services, acupuncture– although health services should always be performed by interns- students who are almost ready to be licensed or who are under licensed supervision can perform these duties, massages, and meals.

Trading

Trade in old books, CDs, and DVDs with friends or acquaintances when you are through enjoying them. It might be a new CD given to that friend or acquaintance or vice versa.

TV and/or DVD/Blu-Ray Player

When shopping for a TV or DVD/Blu-Ray player, try shopping at a TV Repair Shop. Sometimes appliances are brought in to be repaired but were never picked up after the allotted time passed. The repair shop usually sells these appliances for the amount due on them and not the actual cost of the item. What a bargain! Imagine paying only a repair cost of a TV or DVD player that will be new to you.

101 Frugal Tips How to save money and live a minimalistic life

MONEY

ATM Service Charge

Use an ATM machine only once for the week so that it is easier for you to track your withdrawals and also, if there are ATM charges or service charges, then there is a onetime charge instead of having to pay about 2-3 times per week (depending on how many times you would normally do this).

Some banks will not charge an ATM charge or service charge. Shop around until you find a bank that will not charge an ATM charge or a service charge. There are also banks that offer free checking with free ATM cards.

Checks

Never purchase checks from your personal bank. Their prices are usually higher than if you buy them from a mail order company. Mail order check companies are usually advertised in magazines or online.

Credit Cards

Use a fee-free credit card with rewards. When using

a credit card, charge everything to this card to get the rewards from it. But only do this if you are good about paying it off every single month so as not to incur interest on the amount owed. If you pay interest, it isn't worth having the card at all.

Credit Unions

Credit Unions offer the same benefits and services that regular banks do: Get a checking account, buy a certificate of deposit, and/or get a loan. Some will even sell stocks and offer safe deposit boxes. One big perk with taking your business to a credit union instead of a bank is that you can expect to receive a higher interest rate on your savings account while paying a lower rate on your credit cards and loans.

Direct Deposit

Deposit paychecks into your bank account via direct deposit so you will not incur a fee each time you need to cash out your paycheck. Some banks will give extra benefits for doing this small service of using direct deposit.

Interest

Any money that is sitting in a bank is getting some sort of interest. Remember, after a time, interest will stop accumulating on money because interest has been matured. Check the bank for the timeline of interest maturity so your money will not stop growing.

Stocks

Stocks are a good way to make money. Anyone can be a stock broker. The art here is being patient; be alert to changes in current, local, and worldwide news and, of course, getting the right trades of the day.

SHOPPING

Coupons

Clip and use coupons religiously. Get the weekly sales circulars from different stores or from online coupon places, then buy the items that are on sale in the circulars. Watch the weekly sales ads because free items are often times promoted in them.

Some major pharmacies now have the ability to load coupons onto their loyalty cards to make it easier for consumers to shop with them.

Some stores will double coupons. Ask your regular shopping stores for their coupon policies.

Coupons are also a great way to try new things. You would not normally buy an item, but if the item is ½ off, you might be willing to try it.

Discount Stores

Discount stores, such as TJ Maxx, Burkes Outlet, Burlington Coat Factory, Ross, Filene's Basement, Rich's, and Marshalls, are stores that are within a frugal person's budget. These stores will offer items that once occupied the racks of huge department stores, designer stores, and other stores. But the prices are at a lower range because these items might be out of season or even discontinued.

Floor Models

If there is a price difference, buy floor models when it is possible to do so. Floor models often do have cosmetic damages- such as missing knobs, dents, or scratches. However, be aware of this fact before leaving the store. Most times these floor models do not have a warranty and are not returnable or refundable.

Hair Products

Buy hair products from a beauty supply store, which is a store that generally supplies salons with their products. These stores will carry a wide array of products with comparable prices and functions. Buy the beauty care products in bulk which could then save you time and money. Do this instead of buying hair products from the drugstore or supermarket. It is a lot cheaper over time to buy the salon size bottles most times.

Pawn Shops

Pawn shops can be used to buy stuff that seems

unaffordable at that time. How about that guitar that you wanted but you cannot afford to buy? Buy a used one from the pawn shop and twang away, until you are proficient. Now, you may want to get a new guitar, unless you are sentimental to the one from the pawn shop.

Payless Shoe Store

Payless shoes and accessories are within a minimal budget, but they are also offered in modern fashions and styles so they won't seem too inexpensive.

Thrift Shopping

Thrift stores are for the frugal; articles of clothing, appliances, electronics, furniture, or books can be bought at a minimum price here. Thrift Shopping can be accomplished by shopping at The Goodwill Store, Salvation Army, and the local "$10 Dollar Store," or one price for any item in store places. Some great eclectic and antique items can also be found in a thrift store.

Warehouse Clubs

Warehouse shopping, such as shopping at Sam's Club or BJ's Club can be wonderful if you want to buy in bulk, or if you have a large family to feed, or a party you need to cater for. A lot of daily staples can be bought in bulk from these warehouse clubs because the daily use justifies the cost. Items such as toilet paper, paper towels, laundry detergent, and dishwashing liquid can be related to as daily staples. Be wary of buying some bulk items, though, such as snack items. The prices of these items are not economical when calculated as single item purchases versus bulk purchases or cost per unit.

HOW TO CREATE A SIMPLE BUDGET

In order to achieve a frugal living or frugal goals, a budget will aid in this process. A budget is the tracking and estimating of all your income and expenses over a period of time (usually monthly or yearly).

To begin this process, track all your expenses for a short period of time, usually for a month. This can be done by keeping all the receipts of your purchases, including small buys, like emergency purchases at a gas station. Do not forget to include payments toward monies owing, such as an automobile loan.

If the budget's ending monthly total comes out with a negative figure, find ways to make cuts, such as cutting out purchasing personal items or avoiding fees for a month. This will assure that your budget will come out with a positive figure. Avoid making impulse purchases as this will always make your budget go over to having a negative figure.

Savings are also included in the simple budget. If Savings are budgeted for and treated as an expense, then it will not be missed while it is growing interest in the bank. This will then create an emergency source of money when it is needed.

At the end of each month, asses your budget, look over the different areas; are you overspending? Are you saving enough? Do you need an extra source of income? If the budget is not balancing, you need to work harder at sticking to the frugal spending plan or rework the budget to reflect your realistic spending habit.

Below is an illustration of a simple budget. Add all expected income from your paychecks and other sources, such as child support for the month. Then, add all your expected expenses, which are monies paid out from your pocket. Subtract expenses from your income and this total will be what is expected to be had at the end of the month if the budget is followed to the dollar amount.

YEARLY BUDGET	JAN	FEB	MAR	APR	MAY	JUN	JUL	AUG	SEP	OCT	NOV	DEC
INCOME:												
SUB TOTAL												
EXPENSES:												
RENT/ MORTGAGE												
INSURANCE, AUTO												
INSURANCE, HOME												
INSURANCE, HEALTH												
INSURANCE, LIFE												
EXPENSES, AUTO												
ELECTRIC/ GAS												
WATER/ SEWER												
TELEPHONE/ CELL												
CABLE/ INTERNET												
CHILD CARE												
GROCERIES												
PERSONAL ITEMS												
ENTERTAINMENT												
CREDIT CARD (S)												
FEES												
LOAN (S)												
MISCELLANEOUS												
SUB TOTAL												
SAVINGS:												
ACCOUNT (S)												
SUB TOTAL												
TOTAL INCOME												
LESS EXPENSES												
LESS SAVINGS												
TOTAL BUDGET												

365 DAYS PENNY SAVINGS CHALLENGE

This is the by far the easiest way to save money. At the end of this challenge, you will net close to $700 from it (approximately $667.95). You will be mindful that every penny counts. Simply save a penny, or pennies, each day for 365 days and your savings will add up. This can be started by saving 1¢ on day one or doing it in reverse and saving $3.65 on day one. Simply do the following: On day one save 1¢, on day two save 1¢ + 1¢=2¢ and, for instance, on day six save 1¢ + 1¢ + 1¢ + 1¢+ 1¢ + 1¢=6¢.

Follow the chart below daily:

365 DAYS PENNY SAVINGS CHALLENGE

DAY 1	DAY 2	DAY 3	DAY 4	DAY 5	DAY 6	DAY 7	DAY 8	DAY 9	DAY 10	DAY 11	DAY 12	DAY 13	DAY 14	DAY 15
1¢	2¢	3¢	4¢	5¢	6¢	7¢	8¢	9¢	10¢	11¢	12¢	13¢	14¢	15¢
DAY 16	DAY 17	DAY 18	DAY 19	DAY 20	DAY 21	DAY 22	DAY 23	DAY 24	DAY 25	DAY 26	DAY 27	DAY 28	DAY 29	DAY 30
16¢	17¢	18¢	18¢	20¢	21¢	22¢	23¢	24¢	25¢	26¢	27¢	28¢	29¢	30¢
DAY 31	DAY 32	DAY 33	DAY 34	DAY 35	DAY 36	DAY 37	DAY 38	DAY 39	DAY 40	DAY 41	DAY 42	DAY 43	DAY 44	DAY 45
31¢	32¢	33¢	34¢	35¢	36¢	37¢	38¢	39¢	40¢	41¢	42¢	43¢	44¢	45¢
DAY 46	DAY 47	DAY 48	DAY 49	DAY 50	DAY 51	DAY 52	DAY 53	DAY 54	DAY 55	DAY 56	DAY 57	DAY 58	DAY 59	DAY 60
46¢	47¢	48¢	49¢	50¢	51¢	52¢	53¢	54¢	55¢	56¢	57¢	58¢	59¢	60¢
DAY 61	DAY 62	DAY 63	DAY 64	DAY 65	DAY 66	DAY 67	DAY 68	DAY 69	DAY 70	DAY 71	DAY 72	DAY 73	DAY 74	DAY 75
61¢	62¢	63¢	64¢	65¢	66¢	67¢	68¢	69¢	70¢	71¢	72¢	73¢	74¢	75¢
DAY 76	DAY 77	DAY 78	DAY 79	DAY 80	DAY 81	DAY 82	DAY 83	DAY 84	DAY 85	DAY 86	DAY 87	DAY 88	DAY 89	DAY 90
76¢	77¢	78¢	79¢	80¢	81¢	82¢	83¢	84¢	85¢	86¢	87¢	88¢	89¢	90¢
DAY 91	DAY 92	DAY 93	DAY 94	DAY 95	DAY 96	DAY 97	DAY 98	DAY 99	DAY 100	DAY 101	DAY 102	DAY 103	DAY 104	DAY 105
91¢	92¢	93¢	94¢	95¢	96¢	97¢	98¢	99¢	$1.00	$1.01	$1.02	$1.03	$1.04	$1.05
DAY 106	DAY 107	DAY 108	DAY 109	DAY 110	DAY 111	DAY 112	DAY 113	DAY 114	DAY 115	DAY 116	DAY 117	DAY 118	DAY 119	DAY 120
$1.06	$1.07	$1.08	$1.09	$1.10	$1.11	$1.12	$1.13	$1.14	$1.15	$1.16	$1.17	$1.18	$1.12	$1.20
DAY 121	DAY 122	DAY 123	DAY 124	DAY 125	DAY 126	DAY 127	DAY 128	DAY 129	DAY 130	DAY 131	DAY 132	DAY 133	DAY 134	DAY 135
$1.21	$1.22	$1.23	$1.24	$1.25	$1.26	$1.27	$1.28	$1.29	$1.30	$1.31	$1.32	$1.33	$1.34	$1.35
DAY 136	DAY 137	DAY 138	DAY 139	DAY 140	DAY 141	DAY 142	DAY 143	DAY 144	DAY 145	DAY 146	DAY 147	DAY 148	DAY 149	DAY 150
$1.36	$1.37	$1.38	$1.39	$1.40	$1.41	$1.42	$1.43	$1.44	$1.45	$1.46	$1.47	$1.48	$1.49	$1.50
DAY 151	DAY 152	DAY 153	DAY 154	DAY 155	DAY 156	DAY 157	DAY 158	DAY 159	DAY 160	DAY 161	DAY 162	DAY 163	DAY 164	DAY 165
$1.51	$1.52	$1.53	$1.54	$1.55	$1.56	$1.57	$1.58	$1.59	$1.60	$1.61	$1.62	$1.63	$1.64	$1.65
DAY 166	DAY 167	DAY 168	DAY 169	DAY 170	DAY 171	DAY 172	DAY 173	DAY 174	DAY 175	DAY 176	DAY 177	DAY 178	DAY 179	DAY 180
$1.66	$1.67	$1.68	$1.69	$1.70	$1.71	$1.72	$1.73	$1.74	$1.75	$1.76	$1.77	$1.78	$1.79	$1.80
DAY 181	DAY 182	DAY 183	DAY 184	DAY 185	DAY 186	DAY 187	DAY 188	DAY 189	DAY 190	DAY 191	DAY 192	DAY 193	DAY 194	DAY 195
$1.81	$1.82	$1.83	$1.84	$1.85	$1.86	$1.87	$1.88	$1.89	$1.90	$1.91	$1.92	$1.93	$1.94	$1.95
DAY 196	DAY 197	DAY 198	DAY 199	DAY 200	DAY 201	DAY 202	DAY 203	DAY 204	DAY 205	DAY 206	DAY 207	DAY 208	DAY 209	DAY 210
$1.96	$1.97	$1.98	$1.99	$2.00	$2.01	$2.02	$2.03	$2.04	$2.05	$2.06	$2.07	$2.08	$2.09	$2.10
DAY 211	DAY 212	DAY 213	DAY 214	DAY 215	DAY 216	DAY 217	DAY 218	DAY 219	DAY 220	DAY 221	DAY 222	DAY 223	DAY 224	DAY 225
$2.11	$2.12	$2.13	$2.14	$2.15	$2.16	$2.17	$2.18	$2.19	$2.20	$2.21	$2.22	$2.23	$2.24	$2.25
DAY 226	DAY 227	DAY 228	DAY 229	DAY 230	DAY 231	DAY 232	DAY 233	DAY 234	DAY 235	DAY 236	DAY 237	DAY 238	DAY 239	DAY 240
$2.26	$2.27	$2.28	$2.29	$2.30	$2.31	$2.32	$2.33	$2.34	$2.35	$2.36	$2.37	$2.38	$2.39	$2.40
DAY 241	DAY 242	DAY 243	DAY 244	DAY 245	DAY 246	DAY 247	DAY 248	DAY 249	DAY 250	DAY 251	DAY 252	DAY 253	DAY 254	DAY 255
$2.41	$2.42	$2.43	$2.44	$2.45	$2.46	$2.47	$2.48	$2.49	$2.50	$2.51	$2.52	$2.53	$2.54	$2.55
DAY 256	DAY 257	DAY 258	DAY 259	DAY 260	DAY 261	DAY 262	DAY 263	DAY 264	DAY 265	DAY 266	DAY 267	DAY 268	DAY 269	DAY 270
$2.56	$2.57	$2.58	$2.59	$2.60	$2.61	$2.62	$2.63	$2.64	$2.65	$2.66	$2.67	$2.68	$2.69	$2.70
DAY 271	DAY 272	DAY 273	DAY 274	DAY 275	DAY 276	DAY 277	DAY 278	DAY 279	DAY 280	DAY 281	DAY 282	DAY 283	DAY 284	DAY 285
$2.71	$2.72	$2.73	$2.74	$2.75	$2.76	$2.77	$2.78	$2.79	$2.80	$2.81	$2.82	$2.83	$2.84	$2.85
DAY 286	DAY 287	DAY 288	DAY 289	DAY 290	DAY 291	DAY 292	DAY 293	DAY 294	DAY 295	DAY 296	DAY 297	DAY 298	DAY 299	DAY 300
$2.86	$2.87	$2.88	$2.89	$2.90	$2.91	$2.92	$2.93	$2.94	$2.95	$2.96	$2.97	$2.98	$2.99	$3.00
DAY 301	DAY 302	DAY 303	DAY 304	DAY 305	DAY 306	DAY 307	DAY 308	DAY 309	DAY 310	DAY 311	DAY 312	DAY 313	DAY 314	DAY 315
$3.01	$3.02	$3.03	$3.04	$3.05	$3.06	$3.07	$3.08	$3.09	$3.10	$3.11	$3.12	$3.13	$3.14	$3.15
DAY 316	DAY 317	DAY 318	DAY 319	DAY 320	DAY 321	DAY 322	DAY 323	DAY 324	DAY 325	DAY 326	DAY 327	DAY 328	DAY 329	DAY 330
$3.16	$3.17	$3.18	$3.19	$3.20	$3.21	$3.22	$3.23	$3.24	$3.25	$3.26	$3.27	$3.28	$3.29	$3.30
DAY 331	DAY 332	DAY 333	DAY 334	DAY 335	DAY 336	DAY 337	DAY 338	DAY 339	DAY 340	DAY 341	DAY 342	DAY 343	DAY 344	DAY 345
$3.31	$3.32	$3.33	$3.34	$3.35	$3.36	$3.37	$3.38	$3.39	$3.40	$3.41	$3.42	$3.43	$3.44	$3.45
DAY 346	DAY 347	DAY 348	DAY 349	DAY 350	DAY 351	DAY 352	DAY 353	DAY 354	DAY 355	DAY 356	DAY 357	DAY 358	DAY 359	DAY 360
$3.46	$3.47	$3.48	$3.49	$3.50	$3.51	$3.52	$3.53	$3.54	$3.55	$3.56	$3.57	$3.58	$3.59	$3.60
DAY 361	DAY 362	DAY 363	DAY 364	DAY 365										
$3.61	$3.62	$3.63	$3.64	$3.65										

DIANE ROSE

ABOUT THE AUTHOR

Diane Rose was born in Hanover, Jamaica on St. Valentine's Day. She grew up in Negril, Jamaica and Bronx, New York. She has lived in many parishes of Louisiana! "I am still figuring out what I want to be when I grow up." She has worked in the hospitality, retail, and medical industries. She is currently studying to be a nurse after obtaining higher learning in hotel management, childcare management, and medical assisting.

Diane Rose currently lives in Florida with her two sons. In her spare time she enjoys reading, crafting– especially jewelry, and cooking. Jamaica Briefly is her first book, showcasing valuable information about Jamaica, the culture, people, history, sports, and national treasures.

Find out more at http://www.amazon.com/-/e/B00JSSSI9U or email at 37degreesaa@gmail.com.